MONEY PSYCHOLOGY = WEALTH FLOW

Practical Path on How the Psychology of Money Propelled My $500 Monthly Income into a $100,000 Monthly Success Story

PHILBERT TUCKER

This BOOK belongs to

_____

_____

From:

_____

Sign./Date: _____

TABLE OF CONTENT

Chapter 3: Applying Practical Money-Making Strategies

Conclusion: Empowering Your Wealth

INTRODUCTION

The Mindful Path to Financial Triumph

This is a trip that goes beyond the limits of traditional financial wisdom, one in which the junction of thinking and money psychology opens the way to incredible prosperity. As you read these pages, imagine yourself not just as a reader, but as a participant in a transforming experience - a guided journey into the worlds of financial knowledge and wealth.

Embracing the Journey

I encourage you to follow me on a journey that covers the whole financial spectrum, from the humble beginnings of a $500 monthly income to the height of a $100,000 monthly victory. This is more than simply a story about statistics; it's about mentality adjustments, smart decisions, and an unshakable dedication to an abundant vision.

A period when a monthly salary of $500 was the norm, barely scratching the surface of financial security. The trip begins inside this narrative setting, and it is defined by difficulties, crucial decisions, and, most importantly, a thorough examination of the psychological intricacies that support financial success.

The Power of Money Psychology

The notion of money psychology, which holds that our thoughts, attitudes, and emotions have a significant impact on our financial outcomes, is central to this tale. As we peel back the layers of this complex interaction between the mind and money, you'll see how harnessing the power of money psychology can transform not only your financial situation but also the essence of your life.

The transition from $500 to $100,000 monthly wasn't just an increase in money; it was a significant shift in thinking. It requires a shift away from limiting ideas, the development of a wealth mentality, and an unwavering pursuit of knowledge and advancement. The tactics and ideas I offer in these pages are more than just theoretical concepts; they are the instruments that helped me overcome financial constraints and achieve unbelievable affluence.

Let us go on this journey together, chapter by chapter, with each part serving as a stepping stone toward our goal of creating conscious wealth.

Your Role on the Journey

Take an active role in your reading. Reflect on your financial situation, question your preconceptions, and accept the mentality adjustments that may catapult you to prosperity. Consider this a dynamic conversation in which your dreams meet practical wisdom.

This is more than just a handbook; it's an invitation to join in the deliberate production of riches. Whether you want to overcome financial restraints, increase your present income, or just raise your financial awareness, the ideas outlined in these chapters are intended to connect with the objectives of every reader.

Personal Commitment to Transparency

In the spirit of honesty, I'll be revealing not just my successes, but also the problems I had along the road. True success is not free of failures; it is about persistence, flexibility, and an unshakable conviction in the possibilities that await.

Through tales, personal observations, and practical activities, I hope to spark a conversation that extends beyond the pages of this book. This is not a one-size-fits-all prescription, but rather a personalized guidance that encourages you to incorporate your circumstances, abilities, and goals into the wealth generation process.

Embrace the Mindful Wealth Journey

Before we begin this significant inquiry, I ask you to have an open mind, to question the status quo, and to accept change. The pages that follow are not simply a retelling of my tale, but rather a shared narrative in which your path interacts with mine.

Are you ready to explore the transformational junction of thinking and money psychology? Let the trip begin, and may the lessons in these pages lead you to a future of financial empowerment and wealth.

CHAPTER 1

REVEALING THE POWER OF MONEY PSYCHOLOGY

This is our adventure to uncover the mysteries of riches via the prism of money psychology. In this chapter, we'll look at the reason for my goal, the critical role of psychology in wealth building, and the significance of setting realistic expectations.

Personal Background and Motivation

Let me take you back to the beginning of my adventure. My desire for financial achievement was motivated by personal events. Whether it was overcoming financial difficulties, experiencing the impact of positive thinking adjustments, or simply wanting a life of wealth, these experiences inspired my desire to investigate the junction of the mind and money.

Understanding psychology's role in wealth creation

We will look at the underlying relationship between our thinking and financial outcomes. This part will take you on an introspective journey, deconstructing your money attitude and discovering limiting assumptions that prevent wealth building. Understanding psychological boundaries is the first step toward removing them.

Setting realistic expectations

The route to prosperity is a marathon, not a sprint. I'll provide insights on the significance of setting realistic expectations. It is about understanding that wealth creation is a process, and success is frequently reached through constant work over time. This section will help you reconcile your expectations with the realities of financial progress.

1.2 The Mind-Money Connection

Now, let's get to the heart of the matter: the complex interplay between our minds and money. We'll go into the depths of your money though, find any hidden limiting ideas, and work on developing a positive wealth attitude.

Exploring your money mindset

I'll discuss my journey of discovering and modifying my money perspective. Through activities and tales, you'll acquire insight into your personal money connection, as well as an awareness of how past events may be impacting your present financial status.

Identifying Limiting Beliefs

We all have views about money that influence our financial decisions. I'll walk you through the steps of recognizing and addressing these limiting beliefs. By doing so, you'll create new opportunities and pave the path for a healthy financial outlook.

Developing a Positive Wealth Mindset

Positive affirmations, visualization methods, and every day practices - I'll show you how I developed a positive riches attitude. This section focuses on developing a mental climate favorable to attracting plenty and financial success.

1.3 Establishing a Foundation for Financial Success

With the foundations in place, it's time to lay a firm basis for financial success. We'll look at goal-setting strategies, visualization activities, and the need for consistency in achieving long-term success.

Goal-setting and Visualization Techniques

I'll describe my experience with defining specified, measurable, attainable, relevant, and time-bound (SMART) financial objectives. Visualization skills were critical in bringing these ideas to fruition, and I'll share practical exercises to help you do the same.

Creating a Personal Money Blueprint

Your financial plan is unique to you. We'll work together to develop a tailored strategy that is consistent with your objectives, values, and resources. This part is all about translating your goals into tangible steps, creating a clear route to financial achievement.

The importance of consistency

Consistency is crucial to realizing your financial goals. We'll go over tactics for keeping constant in your efforts, overcoming challenges, and having a resilient mentality throughout the wealth-building process.

This chapter provides the framework for the transformational journey ahead. Understanding the power of money psychology enables you to traverse the challenges of wealth development with goal and purpose.

Are you ready to discover the secrets hidden within your mind and pave the way to financial abundance?

CHAPTER 2

USING BEHAVIORAL ECONOMICS FOR FINANCIAL GAINS

Welcome to the world of behavioral economics, an intriguing discipline that combines psychology and economics. In this chapter, we'll look at how behavioral economics affects financial decision-making and delve into the complex area of cognitive bias.

How Behavioral Economics Influences Financial Decision-Making.

Understanding how humans make financial decisions requires an understanding of behavioral economics principles. I'll discuss my own experiences with behavioral patterns that had a substantial impact on my financial decisions, bringing light on how these insights might be used to your benefit.

Identifying Cognitive Biases

We all have cognitive biases that influence our judgment and conclusions. We'll deconstruct various biases, from loss aversion to confirmation bias, and look at real-world examples of how they may either hamper or improve financial performance. Recognizing these biases is the first step toward making more sound financial decisions.

2.2 Understanding the Art of Decision-Making

Decision-making is the foundation of wealth generation. In this part, we'll look at tactics for assessing risks and benefits, using decision-making frameworks, and negotiating emotional triggers that might obscure our judgment.

Analyzing Risk and Rewards

Drawing on my own experiences, I'll discuss how I handled risk assessment and assessed possible benefits. We'll look at realistic risk-evaluation tools and procedures to ensure that decisions are balanced and informed.

Using Decision-Making Frameworks

Decision-making does not have to be based on chance. I'll walk you through excellent decision-making frameworks that offer structure and clarity. Whether it's the pros and cons list, decision trees, or the six-hat approach, you'll have the tools you need to make confident judgments.

Navigating Emotional Triggers In Financial Decisions

Emotions have a huge influence on our financial decisions. I'll provide personal tales and solutions for dealing with emotional triggers such as fear, greed, and impatience. Understanding and regulating these emotions allows you to make more sensible and considerate decisions.

2.3 The Psychology of Investment

Investing correctly is an important aspect of wealth growth. This part will walk you through the process of creating a solid investing plan, avoiding emotional traps in trading, and providing real-life examples of successful investments.

Developing an Investment Strategy

My experience in establishing diverse investing plan includes equities, bonds, real estate, and crypto currencies. We'll go over issues to consider, risk tolerance tests, and the necessity of matching your investments to your financial goals.

Overcome Fear and Greed in Trading

Emotions play an important part in trading. I'll share personal tales of overcoming fear and greed, as well as practical advice for trading with a clear mind. By controlling your emotions, you may make more smart and lucrative trading judgments.

Case Studies: Personal Investment Success Stories

Real-life success stories offer crucial insights. These case studies will inspire and guide your own financial decisions.

2.4 Leveraging Social Dynamics to Promote Financial Growth

Collaboration and networking may often lead to increased financial success. This part will look at successful networking tactics, the value of collaborative initiatives, and the necessity of cultivating a supportive financial community.

Networking Strategies for Financial Success

Building a network brings up new opportunities. Practical networking tactics both online and offline, and how they played an important role in my financial path. We'll look at everything from mentoring to collaborations, as well as the numerous possibilities that might occur as a result of excellent networking.

Collaborative ventures and partnerships

Successful cooperation can result in exponential financial development. I have experiences with joint initiatives, demonstrating how partnerships may harness talents, resources, and opportunities for mutual advantage. This will help you locate and develop collaborative ties.

Creating a Supportive Financial Community

A supporting network may offer encouragement, insight, and accountability. Talking about the necessity of developing a financial community, whether through mentorship, mastermind groups, or internet forums. Your network is much more than simply what you know; we'll look at ways to make significant connections.

This chapter is intended to provide you with the psychological insights and practical skills necessary to handle the intricacies of financial decision-making. From detecting biases to mastering the art of investing, you are now equipped to make educated decisions that will push you to financial success.

CHAPTER 3

APPLYING PRACTICAL MONEY-MAKING STRATEGIES

Congratulations on reaching the core of this handbook! In this chapter, we'll go from studying the psychological factors of wealth development to executing actual, individualized money-making tactics. I'll discuss the strategies I used to make significant financial gains, including tips on monetizing abilities, spotting attractive possibilities, and scaling up for tremendous success.

An overview of the strategies employed

Before we get into the specifics, let's go over the several money-making tactics I used. Whether by exploiting personal abilities, clever company initiatives, or passive income streams, each path contributed to my total financial success.

Mentally preparing for wealth creation

A resilient attitude is essential while executing money-making techniques. I'll offer mental preparation tactics that have helped me overcome obstacles, stay focused on my objectives, and handle the uncertainties that come with any wealth-building path.

3.2 Personal Money-Making Techniques

Now, let's look at specialized money-making ideas based on your abilities, hobbies, and strengths.

Monetizing Skills and Talents

Your abilities and talents are significant assets. I'll walk you through the steps of finding marketable abilities, determining demand, and strategically positioning yourself to monetize them. Real-life examples will show how I converted my abilities into cash sources.

Identifying profitable opportunities

Opportunities for wealth development abound, but identifying them needs a keen eye. I'll discuss my experiences spotting and capitalizing on profitable possibilities, whether in new markets, trends, or undiscovered niches. This part will help you notice opportunities where others may not.

Scaling Up: Converting Micro-transactions into Massive Gains

Scaling is the key to achieving exponential growth. We'll talk about how to scale your business, whether that means extending product lines, entering new markets, or automating procedures. I'll explain how I went from small-scale deals to making big profits.

3.3 Strategic Business Ventures

Starting and growing a profitable business is an important road to wealth generation. This part will go over practical strategies for starting firms, increasing profitability through innovation, and adjusting to market shifts.

Launching Successful Businesses

I'll explain my entrepreneurial path, including the obstacles, accomplishments, and lessons learned from starting successful firms. From inspiration to execution, you'll learn how to build a long-lasting business.

Maximizing profitability via innovation

Innovation is an important driver of financial success. I'll discuss ways to create an innovative culture, stay ahead of the competition, and constantly upgrade your goods or services. Case studies will demonstrate the transformative power of innovation on profitability.

Adapting to market trends

Markets are dynamic, and adjusting to trends is critical for long-term success. I'll describe my experiences navigating market transitions, spotting trends, and altering company tactics accordingly. This section will help you anticipate changes and position your endeavors for long-term success.

3.4 Passive Income and Investments

Passive revenue streams ensure financial stability and long-term growth. We'll look at how to build a varied investment portfolio, generate passive income from real estate, and automate revenue streams to achieve long-term financial success.

Creating a Diverse Portfolio

Diversification is a risk-management approach. I'll walk you through the process of putting together a diverse investing portfolio, taking into account asset classes, risk tolerance, and financial objectives. This section attempts to help you understand the world of investing and make educated decisions.

Real Estate Investments and Rental Income

Real estate may be a significant source of passive income. I'll explain my real estate investing experiences, including tactics for property selection, financing, and earning rental revenue. Whether you're a first-time investor or want to grow your portfolio, this section offers practical information.

Automating Revenue Generation

Automation is critical to freeing up time and resources. I will go over practical techniques to automate money production, whether through internet enterprises, affiliate marketing, or other passive income streams. Building processes that work for you allows you to attain financial success with less effort daily.

By the end of this chapter, you will have a thorough grasp of the practical tactics used in achieving financial success. From monetizing abilities to smart investments, you now have the means to adopt individualized money-making plans and make considerable progress toward your financial goals.

CONCLUSION

Empowering Your Wealth Journey

As we complete this transforming book, I want to thank you for accompanying me on this journey of conscious wealth building. We've worked together to negotiate the complex interplay between money and psychology, apply behavioral economics ideas, and develop realistic, tailored tactics for earning $100,000 in one month.

Your path to financial success is more than just amassing wealth; it's a comprehensive endeavor that includes mentality transformations, smart decision-making, and the application of a variety of moneymaking tactics. Let us highlight the important lessons that capture the spirit of this tutorial.

1. Mind-Money Connection: The Foundation of Wealth.

Understanding the power of your money attitude is the first step toward achieving financial success. You construct the foundations for dramatic change by detecting and altering limiting beliefs, fostering a positive wealth mentality, and establishing a successful foundation via practical goal-setting.

2. Behavioral Economics: The Art of Decision-Making

In the field of behavioral economics, we investigated the complexities of decision-making. Recognizing cognitive biases, assessing risks and rewards, and overcoming emotional triggers are all necessary abilities for making informed and reasonable financial decisions. The psychology of investment offered insights for building a strong investment plan and managing the intricacies of financial markets.

3. Practical Money-Making Strategies: Bringing Dreams to Reality

In the last chapter, we moved from theory to practice, looking at individual money-making strategies, smart company endeavors, and passive income streams. Many ways to generate considerable revenue were explored, including monetizing your abilities, recognizing attractive possibilities, scaling up, creating successful enterprises, and strategically investing in real estate.

Empowerment via Collaboration and Community

Recognizing the power of cooperation and community, we discussed successful networking tactics, the benefits of joint projects, and the significance of creating a supportive financial community. In a world where success is frequently dependent on interwoven relationships, your network becomes a vital asset.

A future of financial empowerment awaits you

As you finish this course, remember that your financial journey is unique. Accept the ideas taught here, apply them to your situation, and see obstacles as chances for progress. Wealth development is an ongoing process, and your dedication to a thoughtful and deliberate strategy prepares you for long-term success.

Continue to learn, adapt, and innovate. Celebrate your achievements, learn from losses, and persevere in your quest for financial success. Remember that the most effective wealth-building initiatives are based not just on financial knowledge, but also on an attitude of abundance, resilience, and continual development.

Your journey to financial empowerment will be paved with wealth, knowledge, and fulfillment. Your adventure has only begun, and the opportunities for wealth creation are limitless. Here's to financial prosperity and a prosperous future!

PRACTICAL NOTES

PRACTICAL NOTES

PRACTICAL NOTES

PRACTICAL NOTES

PRACTICAL NOTES

PRACTICAL NOTES

PRACTICAL NOTES

PRACTICAL NOTES

www.ingramcontent.com/pod-product-compliance
Lightning Source LLC
Chambersburg PA
CBHW071216290526
45796CB00008B/259